Author: Nicole Fenner
Illustrated: Abira Das
Copyright (c) 2019 by Sister Girl Publishing
All rights reserved. This book or any portion thereof may not be reproduced or used in any manner whatsoever without the express written permission of the publisher except for the use of brief quotations in a book review.

Printed in the United States of America
ISBN: 9781730936548

Sister Girl Publishing
PO BOX 811 Halifax,NC 27839
Info@sistergirlcollection

My imagination guides me to the true passion of my heart.

I love learning how to ride a bike with my dad.

My mom taught me how to sew this awesome dress. I love learning new things.

I love eating dinner with my family and talking about my day at school.

I love exercising with my friends.

I love to achieve my goals.

I can be a principal ballerina like Misty Copeland.

I can be a Grand Slam tennis champion like Venus and Serena Williams.

I can be an engineer, physician and NASA astronaut like Mae B. Jemison.

I can be aviator like Bessie Coleman.

I can be a poet and author like Maya Angelou.

I can be an award-winning talk show host like Oprah Winfrey.

I can sing heartfelt songs like Nina Simone.

I can be an Olympic gold medal gymnast like Dominique Dawes.

I can be a NASA mathematician and physicist like Katherine Johnson.

I love new adventures.

I am a beautiful and smart princess.

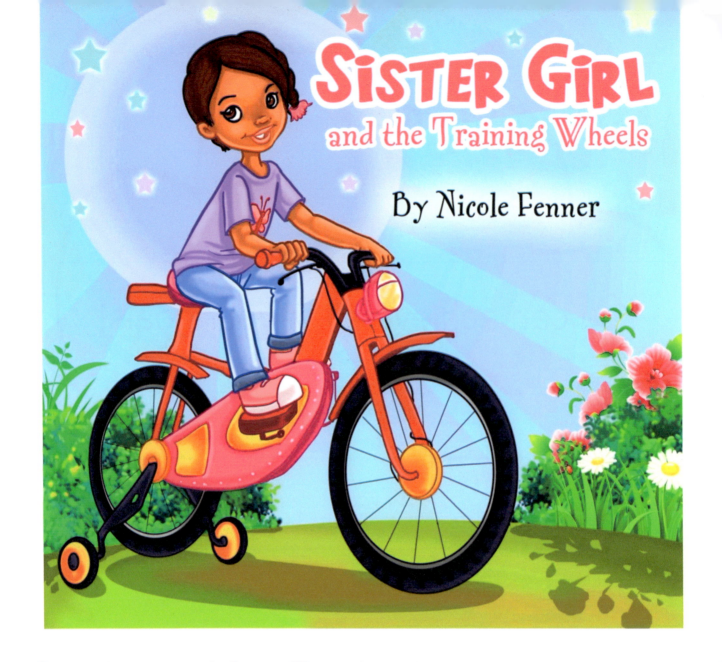

The Sister Girl Collection is an empowerment book series that encourage young children to be courageous, creative, and live productive lives.

 @sistergirlcollection   @sistergirl_coll

 @sistergirlcollection   @sistergirl_coll

www.sistergirlcollection.com

Made in the USA
Columbia, SC
03 June 2024